We

MW00964538

by Edward Fendler
illustrated by Javier Gonzalez Burgos

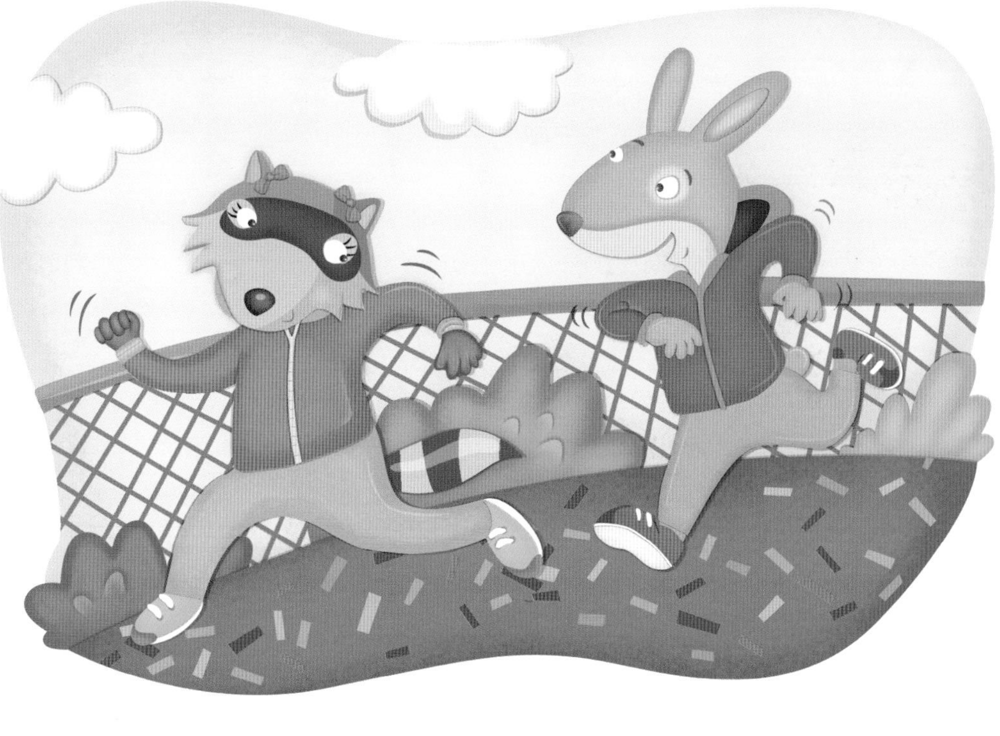

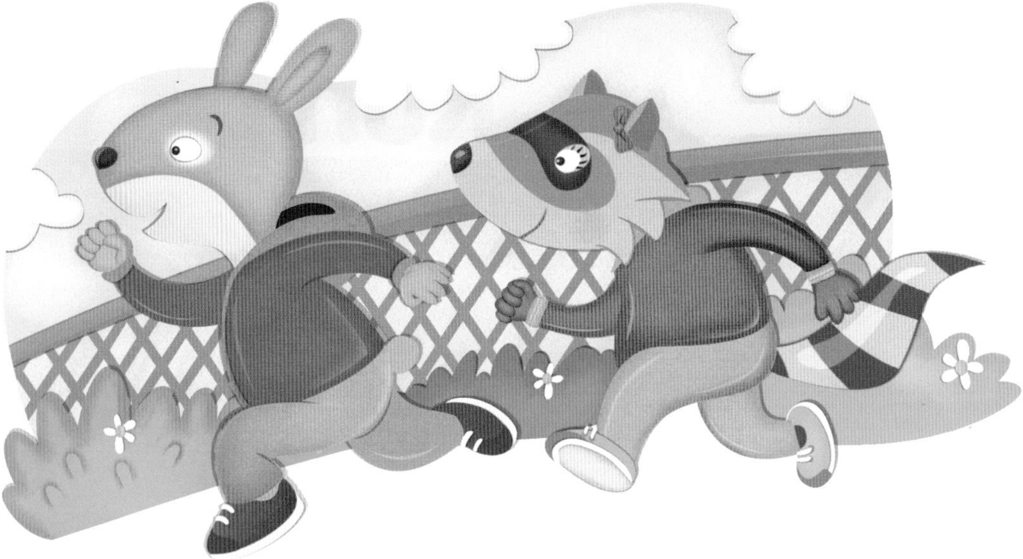

We run.

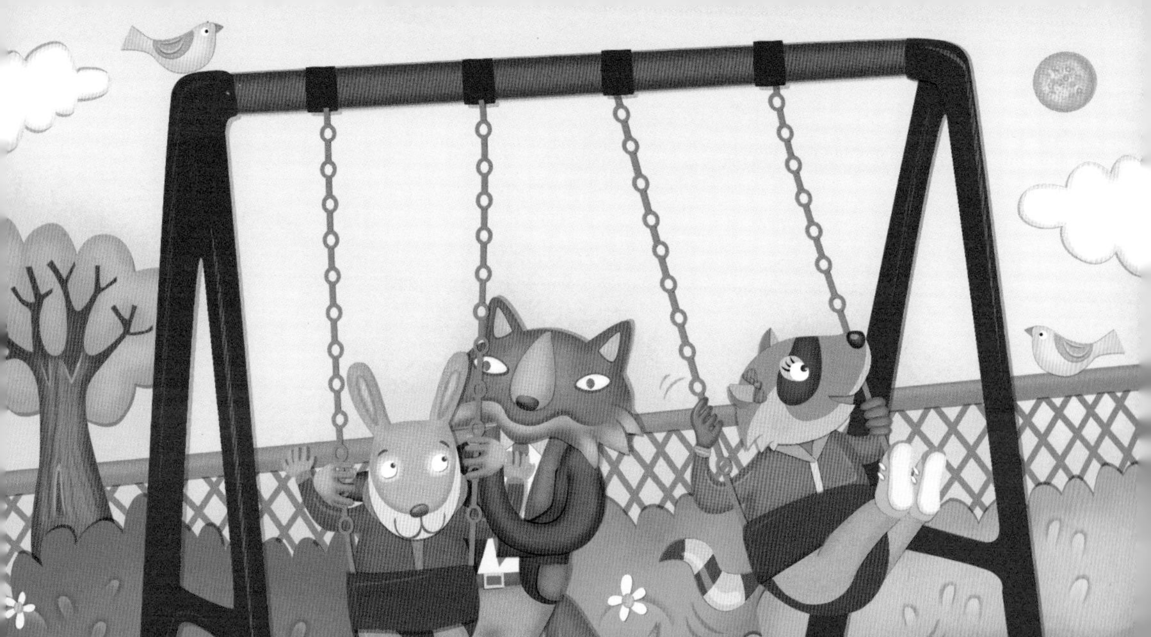

We run to the 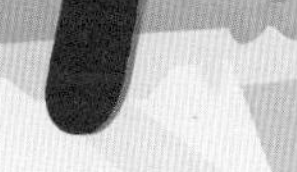 .

swings

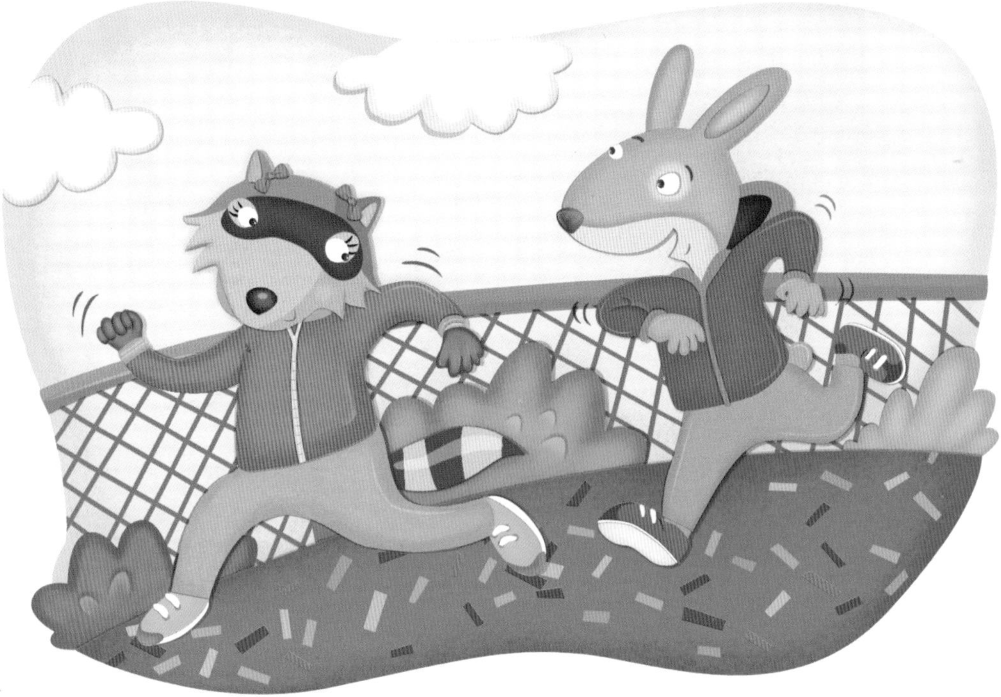

We run.

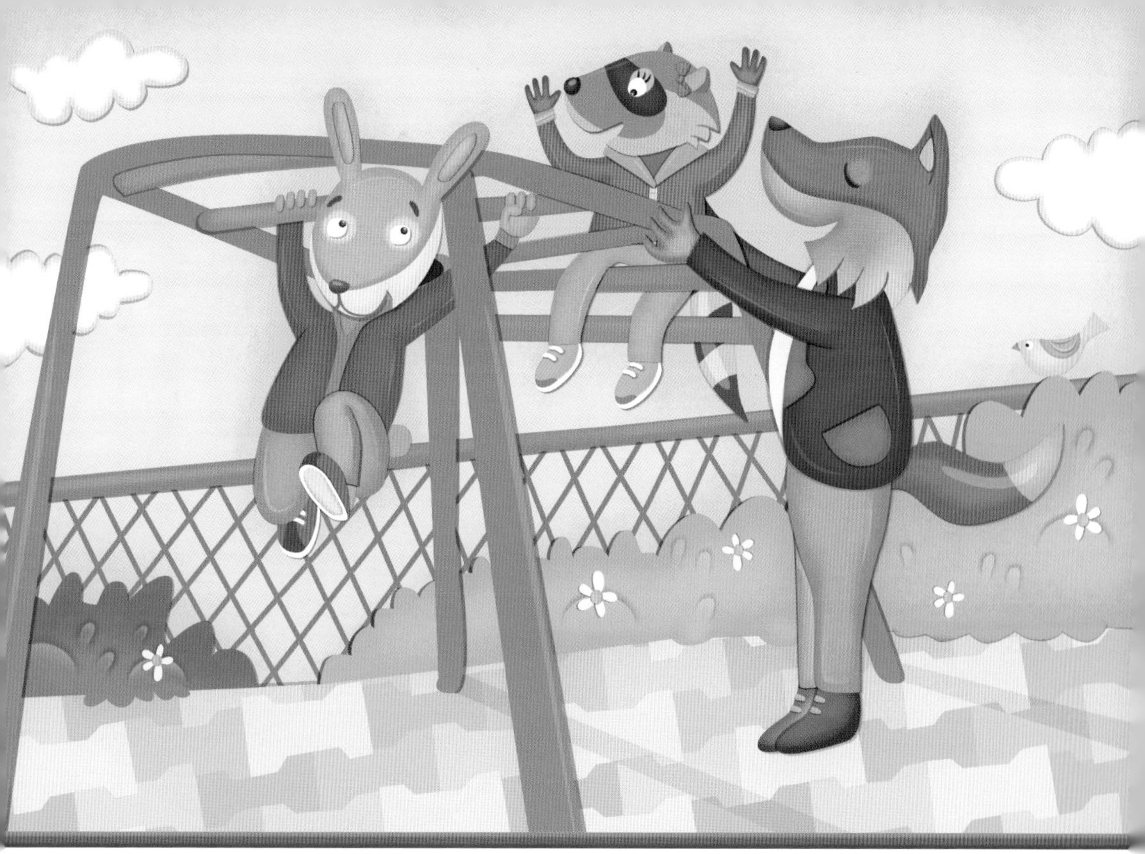

We run to the 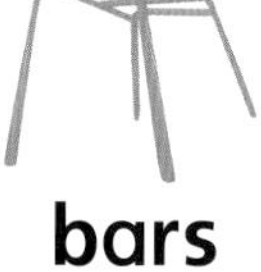 .

bars

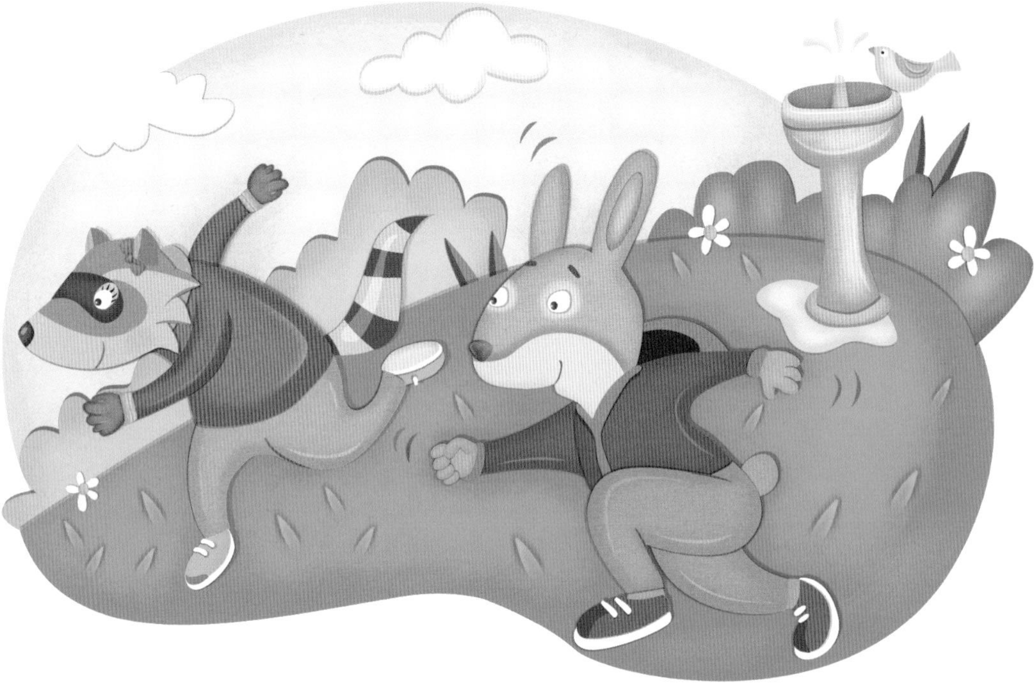

We run.

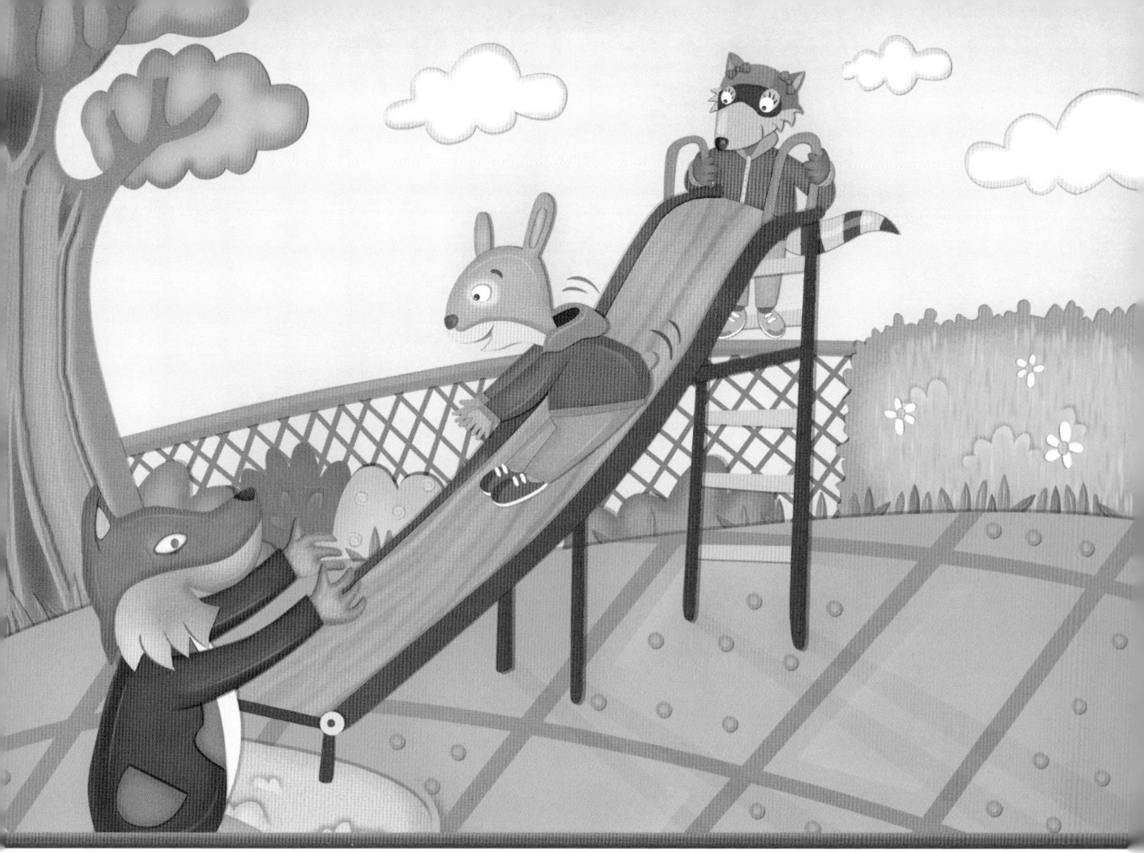

We run to the 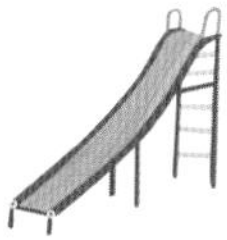 .

slide

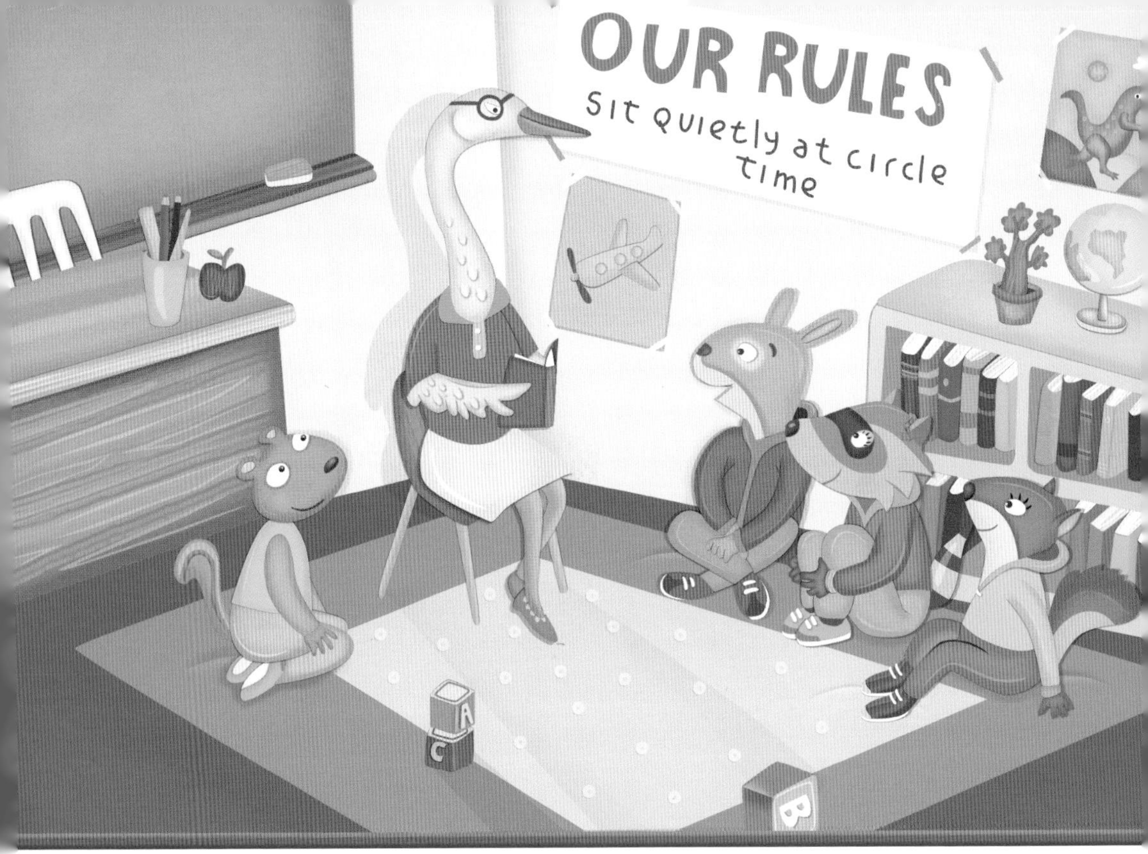

We sit!